Speed Up Your Harvest!
(Revised Edition)

Christy Tola

Library of Congress Number: 2012956427
ISBN: 9789729240867

Unless otherwise indicated all Scriptures
Quotations are taken from the New King James
Version of the Bible.

Part of the Proceeds Will Go Towards
Talent Awareness Program for Youth &
Unemployed Graduates.

Christy Tola Arts & Books
P O Box 4243
Oak Park
IL 60304. USA.

Table of Contents

Introduction 5

Chapter 1
Walking in Love 8

Chapter 2
Faith 13

Chapter 3
Obedience 20

Chapter 4
Knowledge of the Scriptures 24

Chapter 5
Worship 31

Chapter 6
Divine Calling 35

Chapter 7
Divine Location 40

Chapter 8
Relationships 45

Chapter 9
Serve 51

Chapter 10
Conclusion 54

Is Your Soul Saved? 58

Spiritual Guides for Hearing from God 63

Blank Pages for Scriptures 65

Contact Details 75

Introduction

As Christians, we have been taught countless times about the importance of giving our Tithes and Offerings in our local Churches. God promised us in Malachi 3:10 that we should;

"Bring all the tithes into the storehouse,
That there may be food in My house,
And try Me now in this,"
Says the LORD of hosts,
"If I will not open for you the windows of heaven
And pour out for you such blessing
That there will not be room enough to receive it."

He backed His promises in Isaiah 55:10-11 as follows:

"For as the rain comes down,
and the snow from heaven,
And do not return there,
But water the earth,
And make it bring forth and bud,
That it may give seed to the sower
And bread to the eater,
So shall My word be that goes forth from My mouth;
It shall not return to Me void,
But it shall accomplish what I please,
And it shall prosper in the thing for which I sent it."

5

From the above Scriptures, it's clear that when we sow our seed, harvest must follow. It's God's promise.

Also, in Hebrews 11:6, the Bible says,

"...He is a rewarder of those who diligently seek Him."

The questions that we need to consider now are;

i. Why are some Christians still struggling after they've given their Tithes and Offerings to their local Churches and to other good causes?

ii. Secondly, why are some not reaping the way that they should from the seed that they have sown?

iii. Thirdly, if the Bible says, *"...He is a rewarder of those who diligently seek Him"* (Hebrews 11:6), why are some faithful Christians still experiencing 'droughts' in some areas of their lives?

Answers to the above questions and other important information are discussed in this book.

Let's look at this illustration; when farmers sow their seed, they have to water and add fertilizers to the soil and other things that are necessary for the seed to grow. Similarly, there are some spiritual conditions that must be met for our seed to grow and produce a harvest, and for every area of our lives to bear fruit. Some of the conditions are:

Walking in love
Believing by faith
Studying of the Scriptures
Associating with the right kind of people, and so on.

It's my prayer that your obedience to make some changes in your life will cause the processing of the seed that you have sown to be divinely accelerated by God, so that your long-awaited harvest is released quickly, and your life is fruitful. I also pray that you will soon be rewarded for your diligence and faithfulness as you serve the Lord. In Jesus name. Amen.

God bless you.

Christy Tola.

Chapter One

Walking in Love

One of the most important things that Christians must do is to walk in love.

"…If you bring your gift to the altar, and there remember that your brother has something against you, leave your gift there before the altar, and go your way. First be reconciled to your brother, and then come and offer your gift" Matthew 5:23-24.

Also, 1 John 2:9 says,

"He who says he is in the light, and hates his brother, is in darkness until now."

As a devoted Christian, I have found out that some of the things that we sometimes consider as unimportant are not overlooked by God. For example, when we treat others lesser, or we are disrespectful to adults and authority, being disorderly, late to places, prideful, and so on. These attitudes and some others, which I cannot elaborate on at this time, can count against us, if we do not make the necessary changes. Note this; changes will begin to occur once your eyes are opened to the things that are delaying your progress.

From the Scriptures and some of my life experiences, unforgiveness seems to top the list of all the works of flesh, that can adversely affect our prayers, and slow down our progress. Let's look at Matthew 5: 23-24 again,

"...If you bring your gift to the altar, and there remember that your brother has something against you, leave your gift there before the altar, and go your way. First be reconciled to your brother, and then come and offer your gift".

The above Scripture says that we must make up with our brother (or sister) first, before presenting our Tithes and Offerings, or any other gifts at the altar. Therefore, if you are the type that is easily offended, try all your best to control your anger and forgive people quickly. This is because, this attitude will expose you to your spiritual enemies and many things can go wrong anytime we are not under the protective covering of the Anointing.

From what the Holy Spirit has revealed, we are designed like houses, with spiritual doors and windows-our ears, eyes, and mind are windows.

When we study the Scriptures, praise, worship and pray to God, the Anointing comes, cleanses and nourishes us, as well as acts as our spiritual 'Body Guard' (because He surrounds our Spiritual Doors and Windows). We are better protected (as well as all our stuff), because the Anointing prevents unclean spirits from entering our life.

But if we are in unforgiveness or in any other act of the flesh, we will be exposed to them because we have temporarily 'lost' the Anointing that is supposed to shield us. This is because we have indirectly made it easy for our enemies to access the area that they are not supposed to access.

As earlier said, when we pay our tithes or give our offerings, God wants to fulfill His promises to us as written in the Scriptures. But some of our negative attitudes and works of flesh can slow down the process or prevent the full manifestation of our harvest.

"Bring all the tithes into the storehouse,
That there may be food in My house,
And try Me now in this,"
Says the LORD of hosts,
"If I will not open for you the windows of heaven
And pour out for you such blessing
That there will not be room enough to receive it"
Malachi 3:10.

Therefore, it's important to avoid rift with people and make up with those that you disagree with as quickly as possible. Also, devise ways of dealing with 'difficult-to-please' people.

If you are sensitive to the Holy Spirit, He will reveal other areas of your short-comings that can seriously affect your progress. It's in our best interest to walk in love in order to speed up our harvest. Use the Scripture below to pray for strength if you are struggling in the area of forgiving people easily:

"He gives power to the weak,
And to those who have no might He increases strength"
Isaiah 40:29.

Also, meditate on the Scripture below as often as possible:

"If it is possible, as much as depends on you, live peaceably with all men" Roman 12:18.

If you walk in love, you will speed up your harvest.

Chapter Two

Faith

"But without faith it is impossible to please Him, for he who comes to God must believe that He is, and that He is a rewarder of those who diligently seek Him"
Hebrews 11:6.

Faith is the power required to draw God into our situation. It's an important spiritual condition that must be met in order to have access to all the Resources and Provisions in the Kingdom of God.

To believe for things from God, we must truly believe the above Scripture. Let's look at things this way; if you believe that God made the trees, grasses, animals, the seas, rocks, stones, sand and so on, as well as gave people wisdom to make cars, aircrafts, clothes and many other things, this should make Him to be more real to you and boost your faith!

"...Blessed are those who have not seen and yet have believed" John 20:29.

Many times, we have heard the Lord Jesus Christ used this phrase in several verses of the New Testament, *"your faith has made you well."* For example, in the Book of Matthew Chapter 9:22, Jesus said,

> *"Be of good cheer, daughter; your faith has made you well. 'And the woman was made well from that hour.'"*

Also, in the Book of Mark 10:52, the Scripture says,

> *"Go your way; your faith has made you well. And immediately he received his sight and followed Jesus on the road.'"*

This means that what we want to see happen in our life depends on our faith.

Now let's look at a specific example of where faith is at work in the Bible. In Mark Chapter 9, there was a man who brought his son to the disciples of Jesus Christ but had no faith to believe that his son could be healed by them. He then went to appeal to the Lord Jesus to strengthen the child:

> *"…One of the crowd answered and said, "Teacher, I brought You my son, who has a mute spirit. And wherever it seizes him, it throws him down; he foams at the mouth, gnashes his teeth, and becomes rigid. So I*

spoke to Your disciples, that they should cast it out, but they could not." He answered him and said, "O faithless generation, how long shall I be with you? How long shall I bear with you? Bring him to Me." Then they brought him to Him. And when he saw Him, immediately the spirit convulsed him, and he fell on the ground and wallowed, foaming at the mouth.

So He asked his father, "How long has this been happening to him?"

And he said, "From childhood. And often he has thrown him both into the fire and into the water to destroy him. But if You can do anything, have compassion on us and help us."

Jesus said to him, "If you can believe, all things are possible to him who believes."

Immediately the father of the child cried out and said with tears, "Lord, I believe; help my unbelief!"
Mark 9:17-24.

If we can believe that God will indeed supply all our needs, then, whatever we are believing Him for, if it's in His will, will surely come to pass. Lack of faith will hinder us from receiving from God.

Malachi 3:10 says,

"...Try Me now in this," Says the LORD of hosts, " If I will not open for you the windows of heaven

And pour out for you such blessing
That there will not be room enough to receive it."

Also, your circumstances should not determine your walk of faith with God. This is where your maturity as a Christian will be tested.

"He who observes the wind will not sow, and he who
regards the clouds will not reap"
Ecclesiastes 11:4.

If you think about your circumstances, your ability to give in the house of God and to other good causes will be affected. Always look to God and not your circumstances.

Furthermore, try your best not to allow your lack of faith to make you to begin to do things that the Lord said He dislikes. For example, when you start to complain after you've given your Tithes or Offering in your local Church from the little that you have. This can adversely affect your harvest. Start to give thanks to God whenever you notice you are about to start complaining, and don't give under pressure because God loves cheerful givers.

"So let each one give as he purposes in his heart,
not grudgingly or of necessity;
for God loves a cheerful giver"
2 Corinthians 9:7.

16

"Give, and it will be given to you: good measure, pressed down, shaken together, and running over will be put into your bosom. For with the same measure that you use, it will be measured back to you" Luke 6:38.

It's also important to edify yourself by constantly speaking the word of faith whenever you perceive spiritual weakness in this area of your life. Please say the Scripture below repeatedly and use it to pray for spiritual strength.

"He gives power to the weak,
And to those who have no might He increases strength"
Isaiah 40:29.

Strive to prevent sin because sin will hinder you from going confidently to ask for things from God.

"Let us therefore come boldly to the throne of grace, that we may obtain mercy and find grace to help in time of need" Hebrews 4:16.

He who made all things is also able to do what you are asking for, and much more. This should make you to be excited!

> *"Now to Him who is able to do exceedingly*
> *abundantly above all that we ask or think,*
> *according to the power at works in us"*
> Ephesians 3:20.

Exercising your faith more will speed up your harvest.

Chapter Three

Obedience

Your obedience is very important in your spiritual walk with God. This will also help you in other areas of your life. In Malachi 3:10, the Scripture says,

> ""Bring all the tithes into the storehouse,
> That there may be food in My house,
> And try Me now in this,"
> Says the LORD of hosts,
> "If I will not open for you the windows of heaven
> And pour out for you such blessing
> That there will not be room enough to receive it."

From the above Scripture, we are commanded to give our Tithes to our local Church. When we follow simple instructions, we will reap the reward.

I believe that you have read the story of Abraham in Genesis Chapter 22. He's a very good example for illustrating the lessons of obedience;

> "Now it came to pass after these things that God tested Abraham, and said to him, "Abraham!"

And he said, "Here I am."

Then He said, "Take now your son, your only son Isaac, whom you love, and go to the land of Moriah, and offer him there as a burnt offering on one of the mountains of which I shall tell you".

So Abraham rose early in the morning and saddled his donkey, and took two of his young men with him, and Isaac his son; and he split the wood for the burnt offering, and arose and went to the place of which God had told him. Genesis 22:1-3.

(Please make an effort to read the full story).

Abraham did not think about his situation (Isaac was his only son). He just obeyed. Let's see the result of his obedience;

Then the Angel of the LORD called to Abraham a second time out of heaven, and said: "By Myself I have sworn, says the LORD, because you have done this thing, and have not withheld your son, your only son—blessing I will bless you, and multiplying I will multiply your descendants as the stars of the heaven and as the sand which is on the seashore; and your descendants shall possess the gate of their enemies. In your seed all the nations of the earth shall be blessed, because you have obeyed My voice." Genesis 22:15-18.

21

If we do as God has commanded us, we will be blessed like Abraham.

Please meditate on the Scriptures below:

"If you are willing and obedient,
You shall eat the good of the land" Isaiah 1:19.

"So shall My word be that goes forth from My
mouth; It shall not return to Me void,
But it shall accomplish what I please,
And it shall prosper in the thing for which I sent it"
Isaiah 55:11.

Therefore, if you commit to tithing and giving your offerings regularly, and diligently follow all other instructions that you've been commanded, the Scriptures below and more of God's blessings will be yours;

"Behold, the days are coming," says the LORD, "When the plowman shall overtake the reaper, And the treader of grapes him who sows seed..." Amos 9:13.

"For thus says the LORD God of Israel: 'The bin of flour shall not be used up, nor shall the jar of oil run dry, until the day the LORD sends rain on the earth"
1 Kings 17:14.

Your obedience to God will speed up your harvest.

Chapter Four

Knowledge of the Scriptures

The Bible is our 'Manual for Living' and contains all of God's promises for our lives. If you are not devoting enough time to your Bible Study, you are likely to miss out on some important information and instructions for your life. You must also make every effort to find out where some important Scriptures are written for future reference, and for dealing with situations. It's therefore mandatory for all Christians to read the Scriptures all the time, and to note the ones that are necessary for dealing with the areas that require attention in their lives.

Let's look at this illustration; When a woman has had a make-over or visits her hair salon, her physical appearance will improve. Let's compare this to our appearance in the spiritual realm; after we have read the Scriptures and worshipped, we will glow and appear to be well-nourished, but if we have not, we will appear dull and malnourished. Let's relate things to the above illustration; the enemies of our Soul can tell the difference between those who have read and those who have not. Those who appear well nourished spiritually will not attract them because of the Anointing that is around them, while those that have not, are easy targets. This is one of the reasons why many Christians are hated by those in the kingdom of darkness. They cannot come close to Christians who are consistent with their Bible Study and worshipping all the time, because of the glory of God that is around them.

> *"The angel of the LORD encamps*
> *all around those who fear Him,*
> *And delivers them"* Psalm 34:7.

One of the aims of our spiritual enemies is to waste. Hence, if the Christians who are malnourished spiritually are attacked by them, they will have no spiritual strength to withstand the attacks, because of lack of God's Presence, as well as receive protection for their stuff. It's therefore important for Christians to read the Scriptures and worship all the time for their spiritual and material protection.

Also, there are many Scriptures that will commit God to helping us financially, and in other important areas of our lives that require changes. We are to search them out, read, confess and meditate on them for our benefits.

Let's look at some examples of Scriptures that we can meditate on regularly:

This Book of the Law shall not depart from your mouth, but you shall meditate in it day and night, that you may observe to do according to all that is written in it. For then you will make your way prosperous, and then you will have good success. Joshua 1:8.

From the above Scriptures, we can see that it's entirely up to us if we want to be prospered by God. Take note of the highlighted phrase;

"you will make your way prosperous."

This means that, if you read and meditate on the Scriptures and follow the instructions as you are led by the Lord, your actions will cause you to be prospered by Him.

Another example is found in Psalm 119:98-100;

"You, through Your commandments, make me wiser than my enemies;
For they are ever with me.
I have more understanding than all my teachers,
For Your testimonies are my meditation.

I understand more than the ancients,
Because I keep Your precepts."

That is, if you read, meditate, as well as keep God's commandments, you will have divine knowledge of things. You can only find out such truths as above, when you are always studying and meditating on the word of God.

Also, in Psalm 1:2-3;

"…His delight is in the law of the LORD,
And in His law he meditates day and night.
He shall be like a tree
Planted by the rivers of water,
That brings forth its fruit in its season,
Whose leaf also shall not wither;
And whatever he does shall prosper."

Also, if you are always meditating and studying the Scriptures, you'll always be guided and not miss your season of blessing. Furthermore, all the talents that God has deposited into your life will manifest, if you read the Scriptures generously and you do this daily. You will also flow in divine ideas and wisdom.

Let me share the story of how I began to create my company Postcards and Posters. One morning, I was reading the book of Ezekiel 47. When I got to verse 12, the Lord said, *"that verse will make a good postcard."* The Scripture Verse says,

"Along the bank of the river, on this side and that, will grow all kinds of trees used for food; their leaves will not wither, and their fruit will not fail. They will bear fruit every month, because their water flows from the sanctuary. Their fruit will be for food, and their leaves for medicine"
Ezekiel 47:12.

I looked at the verse again and my eyes were opened to see the pictures of river, trees, and fruits, on both sides of the river. Later, I was directed to go and take pictures. So, I got my camera and went to a nearby river, took some pictures, and some of the trees and fruits. This was how everything started. Originally, I started to create postcards, but was divinely instructed to create some as posters from other Scripture verses as well.

After the initial experience, I was given more divine ideas from the Scriptures to create more postcards for witnessing to people, a key tool that I require for my Evangelism Ministry.

I want you to meditate on the Scriptures below. Do this for about 15-30 minutes or longer (or as the Spirit leads). Write them on an index card, and jot down the divine information that you will receive:

"Blessed are those who hunger and thirst for righteousness,
For they shall be filled" Matthew 5:6.

"And you shall remember the LORD your God, for it is He who gives you power to get wealth, that He may establish His covenant which He swore to your fathers, as it is this day" Deuteronomy 8:18.

Always begin your Bible Study by confessing the Scripture below:

"…He opened their understanding, that they might comprehend the Scriptures" Luke 24:45.

(It's important to play Gospel Music or sing after reading the Scriptures or meditating).

If you are consistent with your Bible Study, you will speed up your harvest.

Chapter Five

Praise and Worship

Praise and Worship is of great importance in our spiritual walk with God. Doing this consistently will not only help to speed up your harvest, but will also make other important areas of your life to blossom.

Just as we set aside time to read and study the Scriptures, it's also important to set aside time to seek God daily. It's usually best after your Bible Study. A key advantage of praise and worship is that, it opens the Doorway for the Holy Spirit to come! Music is His KEY Pathway to Humans.

I mentioned earlier that the Anointing is our spiritual 'Body Guard,' that protects us from our enemies. However, this is not automatic, as we have to read, praise, worship or adoration, and pray to God, before this can happen. If the Anointing is on us, we and all our stuff are better protected.

The Presence of God is the realm of breakthroughs. We are only able to enter during praise and worship. This is the time that He destroys our strongholds, nourishes us, fills our void, and deposit divine ideas into our lives.

"In Judah God is known;
His name is great in Israel.
In Salem also is His tabernacle,
And His dwelling place in Zion.
There He broke the arrows of the bow,
The shield and sword of battle" Psalm 76:1-3.

Furthermore, when the Anointing is around us, God is able to order our steps concerning our finances. For example, whenever we are out shopping, The Holy Spirit can nudge us to be careful when we are about to waste money on irrelevant things. He's also able to order our steps as to where to sow our seed, how much to sow, and how to manage any divine provisions that He has entrusted into our care. He's not happy when we are wasteful as this can result in decrease in our finances.

Reading some relevant Scriptures before praise and worship is advised. This will make more power to be available for you during praise and worship, and you will feel the impact. Examples of some Scriptures are listed below:

"As the deer pants for the water brooks, so pants my soul for You, O God. My soul thirsts for God, for the living God. When shall I come and appear before God?"
Psalm 42:1-2.

"O God, You are my God; early will I seek You; My soul thirsts for You; My flesh longs for You in a dry and thirsty land where there is no water" Psalm 63:1.
"Rejoice the soul of your servant, For to You, O Lord, I lift up my soul" Psalm 86:4.

The entire Book of Psalm contains hymns and prayers that are also very good for worship, and there are many other relevant ones throughout the Bible. I will suggest that you search and record them in your Scriptures Journal, if you have one.

(In case you currently have no Scriptures Journal, there are some blank pages for recording relevant Scriptures after the last chapter. Please endeavor to get one as soon as possible).

If you commit to praising and worshipping God daily, you will speed up your harvest.

Chapter Six

Divine Calling

The quickest way to your divine destination in life is to find out about your Divine Purpose from God. Once you are aware about your existence on Earth, you must find out what you are supposed to do during your lifetime. The knowledge of your divine calling will help to accelerate the release of all that will be required for your Life Assignments from God.

Most times, our calling has nothing to do with our career. God may want us to build an orphanage, shelters for the homeless, visit other nations to preach the Gospel, and so on. Our career may be just the means to survive temporarily or as seed, until He provides for our Mission(s) in life. This is usually a bigger blessing than what is coming from our normal income for us to carry out our divine assignments.

Let's look at an example from the Bible;

"And she will bring forth a Son, and you shall call His name JESUS, for He will save His people from their sins" Matthew 1:21.

Jesus' Divine Assignment is as highlighted; *to save people from their sins.* But His career was Carpentry (Mark 6:3). For Him to be able to save the Souls of people, He had to move around, and he needed money to do so. Hence, people were supporting and donating to His Ministry (Luke 8:3). Therefore, we must find out what we are supposed to do too, so God can send all the necessary resources that we will need.

Think seriously about the Scripture below:

"Remember now your Creator in the days of your youth..." Ecclesiastes 12:1.

If you do not know your divine assignment, you will be caught up with things that you have no business dealing with. The knowledge of your divine purpose will make you to begin to move in the right direction and it will commit God to guide you, so that you can fulfill it. It will also reduce stress and your journey will be quicker because you are focused and determined to do the will of God.

Another important thing is that God will begin to link you with the people that can help you make your dreams to succeed. Furthermore, you will not waste money on unimportant projects. Many Christians (and some of God's children who are still in the World), have been abundantly blessed, but they need to ask God what He wants them to do with some of the wealth that has been entrusted into their care. If you fall into this category of people, God may have some important things for you to do later in life. Therefore, do all you can to find out about the Mission(s) that He wants you to embark on, and specifically designed for you during your lifetime.

(There are some Guides to help you to hear clearly from God on Page 63).

(There are some Guides to help you to hear clearly from God on Page 63).

> *"In all your ways acknowledge Him,*
> *and He shall direct your paths"*
> Proverbs 3:6.

Also, some people, who have great missions to accomplish in life but have not yet reached the age of maturity to manage divine provisions or man some key positions, can experience delays in some things from materializing. In most cases, the delay is to mature them (processing period).

"…The heir, as long as he is a child, does not differ at all from a slave, though he is master of all, but is under guardians and stewards until the time appointed by the father" Galatians 4:1-2.

I will also like to use this opportunity to mention that, there are many Christians who have great missions to accomplish in life but are not being adequately provided for because of their lifestyles. God has seen that they are likely to use most of the divine provision, if given to them early, on worldly things. Such people may experience some delays in some areas of their lives until they are spiritually matured. As good stewards, care must be taken as to how we manage God's divine provision. We must manage whatever he has entrusted into our care wisely.

As mentioned earlier, ask in your prayers about your divine assignment in life. If you do, God will begin to order your steps and provide for your needs, because you have indicated that you are serious about His Kingdom by your asking. The more zeal you have for the interest of God's Kingdom, the more divine provision will be channeled to you, and more doors will also be opened to you in other areas of your life.

Some people are created to provide for the needs of others. God will provide for the vision as well as meet all their needs as they serve Him. In Jesus name. Amen.

The knowledge of your divine calling early in life will help to speed up your harvest.

Chapter Seven

Divine Location

If you have read the Book of Ruth, you will get a clear picture about the reason why it's important to ask God about everything concerning our lives.

In the Book of Ruth Chapter One, Elimelech left his divine territory and serious consequences followed. After the death of Elimelech, his wife Naomi had to leave the country of Moab, where they relocated to and returned to Judah, their original place of abode. She had heard that the situation in Judah had improved.

"Then she arose with her daughters-in-law that she might return from the country of Moab, for she had heard in the country of Moab that the LORD had visited His people by giving them bread"
Ruth 1:6.

In my opinion, if Elimelech had known what lies ahead of him and his family, he would not have left Judah despite the drought there. The reason why the Lord did not prosper them where they relocated to could be because they were out of His will.

(The above example is used for illustration only. It's not all those who left for another city or country that are out of the will of God, but it's important to ask for divine directions in every area of our lives (Proverbs 3:6)).

A good example of someone who sought divine guide before deciding to relocate to another city is King David in the Bible. He asked before going to Hebron after the death of King Saul. He did not take the advantage of the fact that the LORD had promised him that he would be the next king (1 Samuel 16). When he perceived that it was time for him to leave, he asked the LORD;

"It happened after this that David inquired of the LORD,
saying, "Shall I go up to any of the cities of Judah?"
And the LORD said to him, "Go up."
David said, "Where shall I go up?"
And He said, "To Hebron"
2 Samuel 2:1.

Let's see what happened when David got to Hebron in 2 Samuel 2:2-4;

"So David went up there, and his two wives also, Ahinoam the Jezreelitess, and Abigail the widow of Nabal the Carmelite. And David brought up the men who were with him, every man with his household. So they dwelt in the cities of Hebron. Then the men of Judah came, and there they anointed David king over the house of Judah."

If God has a divine assignment for you, then it's important to ask about your divine location. He cannot fully bless you as He should, if you are in the wrong place.

Do not start to doubt in case you are faced with some challenges in the new place that you've been led to. Be steadfast in your prayers as you are going through the challenges. Hold on because your change will come, as long as you are in the will of God. Constantly re-assure yourself with His promises in the Scriptures and speak the word of faith to yourself. A good example is Deuteronomy 31:6;

"Be strong and of good courage, do not fear nor be afraid of them; for the LORD your God, He is the One who goes with you. He will not leave you nor forsake you."

I will also suggest that, being in the right church can be of great importance to your fulfilling your divine assignment in life. It's important to ask God to lead you to the right Place of Worship. This is because the Pastor of the Church (most likely with similar calling as yours), will be used to instruct and mature you for your divine assignment(s). He or she would have gone through some life experiences that will be used to help you and others.

Please take note of this important point; there is divine provision for every vision from God but staying in the wrong location can sometimes make the promises of God to be of no effect. Please make sure you hear clearly from God before proceeding to any place. If you are where you are supposed to be, the peace of God will guide your mind, no matter the situation that you are faced with (Philippians 4:7).

(There are some Guides on Page 63 that can help you to hear clearly from God).

Being in the right divine location will activate the power of God to speed up your harvest.

Chapter Eight

Relationships

Many Christians have unbelieving relatives and friends that can discourage or prevent them from giving.

"Blessed is the man who walks not in the counsel of the ungodly..." Psalm 1:1.

Many are also in the company of those who are not as spiritually matured as they are. If you withhold from giving to the Lord the way you should, you will rob yourself of your divine blessings because it's a kingdom principle to give and to also receive.

"Give, and it will be given to you: good measure, pressed down, shaken together, and running over will be put into your bosom. For with the same measure that you use, it will be measured back to you" Luke 6:38.

For example, if you are about to give your Tithes or Offerings, any negative comment from your unbelieving relatives or friends can discourage or prevent you from giving generously.

45

In 2 Corinthians 9:7, the Bible says,

"…Let each one give as he purposes in his heart, not grudgingly or of necessity; for God loves a cheerful giver."

Your unbelieving relatives/friends or the spiritually immature ones should not be dictating what you should do when it comes to spiritual matters. This is because you can perceive the things of God better than them. Their negative influence on you can prevent you from receiving your blessings. I pray that you will not be hindered by such friends.

"Do not be unequally yoked together with unbelievers. For what fellowship has righteousness with lawlessness? And what communion has light with darkness? And what accord has Christ with Belial? Or what part has a believer with an unbeliever?"
2 Corinthians 6:14-16.

I want you to learn something from King Saul before he became the king in 1 Samuel 10. He did not reveal or discuss what went on between him and Samuel, and any other Kingdom issues with his uncle. In my opinion, he must have perceived that the man will not understand some things about the Kingdom, because he did not know God, so the Holy Spirit nudged him not to disclose some things to him. Furthermore, he can also be used to cause a hindrance in the life of Saul, who was being prepared as the future king. Therefore, Saul did not say much or seek his opinion.

"…about the matter of the kingdom, he did not tell him what Samuel had said" 1 Samuel 10:16.

(Please read the full story in 1 Samuel 10).

Most of the stories in the Bible are examples of how we should handle any situation that we are confronted with:

"All Scripture is given by inspiration of God, and is profitable for doctrine, for reproof, for correction, for instruction in righteousness" 2 Timothy 3:16.

Also, some of your business partners can be hinderers to your harvest and progress, if you are dealing with those that are spiritually immature. You can be their friends but don't seek their opinion about church related matters and things pertaining to your life. This is because they will use their logical mind to analyze your situation and offer advice as they see things. You should rely on the Word of God.

*"Your word is a lamp to my feet
And a light to my path"* Psalm 119:105.

*"And I will walk at liberty,
For I seek Your precepts"* Psalm 119:45.

Think about this point; how can someone who doesn't read the Scriptures and worship God know the things of God? Therefore, spiritual matters should be dealt with spiritually, by the spiritually matured. Stay close to those who are wise in the things of God. Be around good role models, God-fearing people, and ask God to send the people that will help you to fulfil your divine calling.

"As iron sharpens iron, so a man sharpens the countenance of his friend" Proverbs 27:17.

It's important that you pray for those who are non-Christians among your relatives, friends, and business partners. Pray and speak to them to accept Jesus Christ. If you ask God to help you concerning your relationships, He will remove those that are not supposed to be in your company. Don't be surprised or begin to feel sad if some of your friends are suddenly leaving after you have prayed, or you're changing your mind about some of them. God will open your eyes if you pray concerning your relationships and those that you are dealing with.

> *"I am a companion of those who fear You,*
> *And of those who keep Your precepts"*
> Psalm 119:63.

> *"Let those who fear You turn to me,*
> *Those who know Your testimonies"*
> Psalm 119:79.

Relying on God's wisdom, through the Scriptures, will speed up your harvest.

Chapter Nine

Serve

Please read the following Scriptures carefully and think about what it says:

"Thus says the LORD of hosts: "Consider your ways! Go up to the mountains and bring wood and build the temple, that I may take pleasure in it and be glorified," says the LORD" Haggai 1:7-8.

Few years ago, while working as a teacher, I suddenly lost my job. Life was very difficult to say the least. I started to pray and ask the Lord what the problem was. One day, as I was reading my Bible, I was led to Haggai 1:7-8. Suddenly, I heard a voice within me that said, *"what you are going through is from the LORD!"*

I immediately asked what I had done wrong and what I should do about my situation. I was instructed to go to the church that I was attending at the time, and volunteer some of my time to serve. I ran to my church and begged one of the members of staff there to give me something to do. I then promised to come back and serve in the church from then on.

Later when I returned home, there were two messages on my answer phone-two jobs were waiting for me! To cut my long story short, I devoted my time to serving in my local church, as I had promised earlier, and many things changed for the better from then on.

I will advise you to commit yourself to serving in your local church and don't waste time doing this, especially if you're currently unemployed.

When you volunteer to serve in your local church, you are sowing a seed towards your future. This will help to speed up your harvest.

Chapter Ten

Conclusion

I know many of you have given your Tithes and Offerings dedicatedly and have been faithful to God in your service to Him but are yet to receive the harvest that you deserve. I want you to pray and ask God to open your eyes to the areas of your life that require some changes and take heed to your ways.

It's time for Christians that are going through financial challenges and difficulties in other areas of their lives to pay attention to their attitudes, lifestyles, and other things that may be responsible for the delay of their harvest.

"My people are destroyed for lack of knowledge"
Hosea 4:6.

Also, many people have divine assignments that have to do with caring for others. If you seek God concerning the things that will help you to take care of the need of others, God will not only do what you are asking for, but give you more than you desire. This is because you have become one of His 'Employees'.

Let's look at this illustration; if you are working for an earthly king, people will see his or her glory around you. Now compare this to working for the KING of Kings, and the LORD of all Lords! There is a special harvest reserved for people who truly have the desire to help others.

"...He who waters will also be watered himself"
Proverbs 11:25.

Furthermore, it's important to have the heart of a Giver. This will make harvest to always meet harvest in your life. We must never forget that we came into this World with nothing and we shall leave with nothing. Therefore, give and share with the needy all the time, as much as you can afford. Please don't forget your relatives too (Isaiah 58:7). Let's emulate the Apostles and be generous with our wealth.

"Now all who believed were together, and had all things in common, and sold their possessions and goods, and divided them among all, as anyone had need"
Acts 2:44-45.

55

"For we brought nothing into this world, and it is certain we can carry nothing out" 1 Timothy 6:7.

Please meditate on the following Scriptures:

"The generous soul will be made rich..." Proverbs 11:25.

"Give, and it will be given to you: good measure, pressed down, shaken together, and running over will be put into your bosom. For with the same measure that you use, it will be measured back to you" Luke 6:38.

I will also suggest that you should try as much as possible to strive to control your spending habits and buy only the things that you need and can afford. As said earlier, God will not be pleased if we are wasteful.

If you are a business owner, try not to overprice your goods and be kind to your fellow brothers and sisters in Christ. People will pronounce more blessings on your business if you are always showing kindness to them.

"Therefore, as we have opportunity, let us do good to all, especially to those who are of the household of faith" Galatians 6:10.

Finally, be creative with your God-given Talents, and make profits from them. Our talents are given to us for some reasons, one of which is to make money. Moreover, God promised to bless the work of our hands in Genesis 28:12. Therefore, find out more about your talents and use them, especially if you are currently unemployed. Please read about the Parable of the Talents in Matthew 25:14-29.

(One of my Books titled *'Make Profits from Your Talents'* elaborates more on how to make use of our God-given Talents to generate extra income. See back of this Book for details on how to purchase a copy).

It's important that you are consistent with your Bible Study, Praise, Worship and Prayers. Do them every day and not only when you have a need (twice daily is better).

"Remember now your Creator in the days of your youth, before the difficult days come…" Ecclesiastes 12:1.

This is the time to strive more and make some important changes in your life because,

"…You have dwelt long enough at this mountain turn…" Deuteronomy 1:6-7.

Is Your Soul Saved?

If you have not invited Jesus Christ as your Lord and Savior, this is the time to do so. This is because you need the help of the Holy Spirit. He is our Guide and Comforter in life. He can only come to you after you have invited Jesus Christ, and when you begin to Study the Scriptures, praise, and worship God. You also need Him to help you to pray.

"…If you confess with your mouth the Lord Jesus and believe in your heart that God has raised Him from the dead, you will be saved. For with the heart one believes unto righteousness, and with the mouth confession is made unto salvation" Romans 10:9-10.

Please say the Prayer below:

Dear Heavenly Father, I am sorry for my sins. Please forgive me. Jesus Christ, please come into my life and help me. In Your name I pray. Amen.

It is important that you follow these Instructions:

Prayer
Pray every morning and ask God to protect and order your steps throughout the day. Also, ask the Holy Spirit to reveal your Divine Purpose to you. As you do, He will begin to order your steps and lead you to where you are supposed to be in life.

Read the Bible and Worship

It's important that you create time for your Daily Devotion with God. When you're about to start your Daily Devotion (twice daily is advised), saying the Scripture below will help you. Also, pray and ask the Holy Spirit to teach you, as you study:

*"...He opened their understanding,
that they might comprehend the Scriptures"* Luke 24:45.

As soon as you become a Christians, you are like a new born baby that requires milk. Likewise, our Souls require spiritual nourishments for it to develop. Therefore, reading the Bible and Praise and Worshipping God will provide the spiritual nourishments that your Soul requires. It will also protect you from 'spiritual infections', ease your pains if you are spiritually afflicted, as well as allow the Holy Spirit to come close and help you.

It's very important that you read the Bible every day but must be accompanied by Gospel Praise and Worship Music, or songs of adoration to God. This will draw the Holy Spirit to your situation quicker. I will advise you to incorporate reading the Book of Psalms during your Daily Devotion.

Reading the Bible generously will also help you to discern spiritual truth about your life and situations.

"I have more understanding than all my teachers,
For Your testimonies are my meditation.
I understand more than the ancients,
Because I keep Your precepts" Psalm 119:99-100.

As you study, get use to writing Scriptures on small/index cards to meditate on, memorize, and confess, during the day. This will help to protect your mind and strengthen you against temptations.

Go to Church and Fellowship
We are commanded to fellowship with other Christians. But it's important to ask the Holy Spirit to lead you to a Church.

"...Let us consider one another in order to stir up love and good works, not forsaking the assembling of ourselves together, as is the manner of some, but exhorting one another" Hebrews 10:24-25.

One of the major reasons for going to Church is because Corporate Anointing is sometimes required for certain breakthroughs and this is only possible in a church environment. You need the prayers of other Christians and the Pastor. (The Bible says, *One person will chase a thousand and two are capable of putting ten thousand to flight;* Deuteronomy 32:30).

Secondly, the Church is the Holy Spirit School and Classroom. This is where He teaches us, His Students. The Pastors/Ministers are His Mouthpiece. You need a good and experienced Pastor that has been trained by the Holy Spirit, especially if you perceive that you have a major mission to accomplish in life. God will use the Pastor of the Church to train you for your future Ministry or Divine Calling for your life. Therefore, it's important that you pray and ask the Holy Spirit to direct you to His choice of Church for you.

Baptism
Get baptized in your local church. Christians are commanded to do so in the Bible;

"...Let every one of you be baptized in the name of Jesus Christ for the remission of sins; and you shall receive the gift of the Holy Spirit" Acts 2:38.

Serve
As soon as you begin to attend your new Church, volunteer yourself as a worker in any of the Ministries. Also, pray for guidance to serve in the area of ministry that will be of great benefit to your future.

Ask for Guidance
It's also important to always ask the Holy Spirit to guide you in everything that you do, so that He can help you to prevent mistakes. You are permitting Him to help you if you ask. God is the Owner of our lives and the Earth that we live in. We will be operating in the dark if we do not pray or acknowledge Him in all our ways, we are likely to make some mistakes, which are preventable.

"The earth is the LORD's, *and all its fullness,
The world and those who dwell therein"*
Psalm 24:1.

*"In all your ways acknowledge Him,
And He shall direct your paths"*
Proverbs 3:6.

Love One Another
Love people as we are commanded and try your best to avoid malice and unforgiveness, so your prayers are not hindered. Use Isaiah 40:29 to pray for help if you're struggling in this area.

"A new commandment I give to you, that you love one another; as I have loved you, that you also love one another. By this all will know that you are My disciples, if you have love for one another" John 13:34-35.

Please remember to share the Gospel with your relatives and friends.

God bless you.

Spiritual Guides for Hearing Clearly from God

(It's important that you have accept Jesus Christ as your Lord and Savior before using the Guides below)

1. Read five or more Chapters of the Book of Psalms
2. Say the following Scriptures as many times as you like:

"In all your ways acknowledge Him,
And He shall direct your paths" Proverbs 3:6.

"I will instruct you and teach you in the way you should go;
I will guide you with My eye" Psalm 32:8.

3. Worship God with your favorite Gospel Praise/Worship Music or sing some songs of adoration to Him
4. Ask your questions in a very simple and direct way.

I will suggest that you should always keep a notepad and pen with you so you can write down the instructions that you will receive from God. He sometimes speaks when we least expected and in any form that He chooses; dreams, visions, intuitions, verbal and so on. He can also send someone to you. It's important that you write the Instruction(s) immediately you hear from Him and do as you are instructed without delay. Exercise your faith and have a heart of expectation to hear from God.

I will advise you to avoid over-eating, especially if it's near your bedtime. This will help you to hear or see God's instructions clearly. Try your best to prevent flesh from interfering with your spiritual life.

Blank Pages for Scriptures

Contact Details:

Christy Tola Arts & Books
P O Box 4243
Oak Park
IL 60304. USA.

Email: contact@tolabooks.com

More information about Pastor Christy Tola @ christytolaministries.org.

Facebook: Facebook.com/Christytolaministries

Youtube: Christy Tola Ministries

Instagram: Christy Tola

Search for Christy Tola's Books @
www.amazon.com

The Paperback Edition of 'Get Cleansed and Fill Your Lamp with Oil' and other Books by Christy Tola are now available at Amazon.com and other leading Bookstores.